KENNETH M.

ADAMS

A RETROSPECTIVE EXHIBITION

Van Deren Coke

With a Foreword by Andrew Dasburg

published by

The University of New Mexico Press, Albuquerque

The University Art Gallery
a department of the College of Fine Arts
The University of New Mexico

    Clinton Adams, *Dean*
    Van Deren Coke, *Director*
    William Thonson, *Designer*
    Frances Hogan, *Secretary*

© THE UNIVERSITY OF NEW MEXICO PRESS 1964

Library of Congress Catalog Card No. 64-17853   *First edition*

Manufactured in the United States of America
by the University of New Mexico Printing Plant

PHOTOGRAPH OF KENNETH M. ADAMS BY VAN DEREN COKE

KENNETH M. ADAMS   A RETROSPECTIVE EXHIBITION

FOREWORD

In thinking of Kenneth Adams and his work, it strikes me that over the many years I have known him, his ruling preoccupation has been with realizing the character and basic form of things seen and loved, expecially people. At no time have I known him to sacrifice human content for an abstract pictorial system, either of a personal or general nature, such as dominates the art of today.

It was here in Taos, in 1924 to 1937, after having studied both in this country and in Europe, that his style matured. During that period the adobe villages of the valley, pueblo Indians, and Spanish colonials still retained much of their special character. Life was simple and down-to-earth. Time had not entirely become the equivalent of money. Adams, like most of us then—and as future artists may again do—painted a variety of subjects selected from the unique environment we enjoyed. For him, some of these were of but passing concern, as his strongest sympathy was for people. Though some of his finest work is of the Indian, the bulk is rooted in the life of the Spanish community. Friends and neighbors, both young and old, posing or busy with their labor, served as subjects for his pictures. In this, I believe he stands alone, in that the older painters of Taos based their painting primarily on the Indian and his affairs.

A selection from the work of Adams' Taos period would constitute an important historical record of the Spanish people of the period. I have in mind such items of superior achievement as *Doña Ascencione in Wicker Chair*, *Benerisa Tafoya*, *The Adobe Maker*, *Old Spanish Woman*, *New Mexican Village*, and *The Harvest*.

In 1937 Adams took up permanent residence in Albuquerque, and began his career as a professor in the University of New Mexico Art Department. As a result of this move, a change took place in his work. It was no longer strongly regional as it was in Taos. He began to concentrate on still-life arrangements, flower pieces, nude figures, portraits, and some striking landscapes. In keeping with the character of the man, these were intimate and personal subjects as opposed to scenes of the city, a subject which does not appear in Adams' oeuvre.

Ken Adams is a painter who deals with the tangible reality of his medium and subjects. The guiding principle on which he builds is the revelation of basic geometric structure in combination with a humanistic view of life. Through pleasurable relations of color to shape, his pictures have formal interest of their own which exists outside of, but in harmony with, the associations we bring to his variety of subjects. His is an art of actuality with allusions to underlying truths.

ANDREW DASBURG

Taos, New Mexico
November 1963

Andrew Dasburg, who first came to New Mexico in 1917 and settled in Taos in 1930, is one of the outstanding pioneers of modern art in America. He has been influential as a teacher and writer as well as a painter. Kenneth Adams has known Dasburg since 1919 when he entered his classes at the summer school of the Art Students League at Woodstock, New York.

INTRODUCTION

Kenneth M. Adams' art is devoted to creating new versions of old themes in a simple straightforward manner. To this end he is concerned with the physical propertics of the visible world. He always renders substance in a way that suggests the concrete materiality of forms, although to compete with nature is not his aim. Visual observations, serving as a source of stimulation, are reduced to more accessible forms and colors without destroying the aura which initially prompted him to put brush to canvas. His imagery conducts us into the presence of an intimately observed world that is both public and private—public in the clarity that is celebrated, private in its promise of deeper fulfillment.

During the four decades he has lived in New Mexico, the art world has been exposed to a half dozen or more new movements. Adams was well aware of these but he refused to be enticed from the path he selected as his own in the early nineteen twenties. It is not that he has a narrow view of art or wishes to counterfeit reality. Rather, he has directed his efforts toward capturing something of the uniqueness which characterizes the people and land of northern New Mexico. His procedure in this respect is different from that followed by many of his contemporaries. While they twisted and turned to the tune of each new artistic revolt and often suffered from vain pursuits of a vogue which was not sincerely felt, he painted in a realistic manner the eternal qualities of certain individuals, landscapes, and flowers. In this quest he did not resort to visual platitudes nor did he seek new departures just to add zest to the familiar aspects of his subjects.

Adams' work derived from a study of the traditions which were established in post-impressionist painting and enriched by fauvism and cubism. From Andrew Dasburg, his greatest single influence, came a concept of realism that incorporates much of Cézanne and the early Picasso. But Adams' view of man and nature springs from an outlook that is his own. He exerts a sensitive control of these well chosen forms. Basic shapes and contours in combination with lustrous color animate his work and give it a distinctive cast.

With his idiom basically established by 1924, he began to probe the spirit of the Indian and Spanish peoples with whom he lived in the Taos region. From the beginning, despite his somewhat conservative mode, Adams definitely broke with the picturesque and sentimental attitudes of the more conventional Taos and Santa Fe painters. In the process he added a new dimension to the same subjects that these painters so often emasculated. An awareness of the inward quality of common things and ordinary people is strongly suggested in his most successful pictures.

From his early, rather loosely painted, French landscapes he evolved a style that became more concise without losing the brilliance of his early color notations. Part of this change was brought about through his association with Dasburg. Other aspects stem from the stylizations used by the Mexican muralists of the twenties and thirties. Although he did not see any original works by the Mexican painters, their style was known to him through photographic reproductions in art periodicals. It was the quality of direct simplicity that he admired most in the Mexican painters' work. In the work of Orozco and Siqueiros he felt there was a sense of real compassion for the human condition, despite the more obvious propaganda content of certain of their paintings. He feels today that there is a great similarity in the humanistic qualities incorporated both in Orozco's murals and Masaccio's frescoes which so impressed him as a young man in Italy. The figures, in their rudimentary construction, transmit a feeling of strength and solemn dignity which harmonized with Adams' own view of man. In the mid-thirties he frequently abbreviated his forms in very much the same way as did the Mexican painters. This quality appears in *The Spring* and *Harvest* paintings as well as in several of his lithographs, such as *Ranchos Church—Moonlight*.

When asked about how pictures like these were painted, Adams replied:

"I have no formula for beginning a painting. I have painted and completed landscapes out-of-doors and I have painted them in the studio from drawings and color notes. At times I have worked both directly from the motif and in the studio on the same canvas. From small pictures I have painted large canvases when I have felt a larger area would make for a better interpretation of the subject. Specifically the painting called *New Mexico Landscape*, which won the 4th W. A. Clark prize at the Corcoran in 1935, was worked on both directly from the motif and in the studio. I first made an 18x20 inch drawing out-of-doors. Then I enlarged this on to a 36x40 inch canvas in the studio. The canvas was taken into the field and worked on directly from the motif until it was developed to a rather advanced state, after which I finished the picture in my studio.

"The 30x40 inch canvas which I call *The Valley* was painted entirely in the studio using my small picture, *The Valley—Rain*, as the motif.

"Genre pictures, such as *Harvest* and *The Spring*, were developed from memory without the use of models. I suppose one might call them syntheses of multiple visual experiences during the years I lived at Taos.

"Portraits such as *Indian Woman and Child, Old Woman, Benerisa Tafoya, Portrait of a Pioneer, Indian Girl with a Basket of Corn, Portrait of Juan Duran* and *Doña Ascensione* were painted directly in oil from models without preliminary sketches of any kind. I composed as I painted."

Adams has done a number of portrait commissions. These were usually developed from preliminary drawings which were made to scale so as to study the order of the composition. The drawings were used only as indications, for he sometimes found it necessary to shift elements after transfer to the canvas. This was necessary because the function of color is difficult to foresee when combined with drawing.

Color has played a major role in Adams' work. He says:

"When I begin painting I usually limit my colors to those I believe are essential to establish the basic color of the largest spatial areas. As work progresses I add colors to my palette only if they are needed. Theoretically, I try to maintain equal progress for all areas of the canvas. In practice this is often very difficult to do. I believe my best work has come about when I came nearest to maintaining this discipline throughout the work from beginning to end.

"It seems to me axiomatic that the fewer pigments one uses the greater the command one should have over them. Delacroix worked with many pigments, Cézanne by comparison, with few, and Renoir with even less. All were great colorists."

Although Adams is still interested in intimate views of the land as well as panoramas, he feels it is much more difficult to find the kind of view which had prompted him to paint in past years. He says:

"I am conscious of change in the contemporary landscape from that of the twenties and thirties and am only beginning to adjust and accept it. Whether or not I can use it for future painting I do not know.

"It seems to me that the landscape of the twenties and thirties is now as obsolete as that of Claude Lorrain's day. There probably are enclaves in

New Mexico that are not bi-sected by paved highways but I doubt if there are any that do not have radio or television antennae projecting from the roofs of at least a few houses."

In addition to his murals and easel paintings, Adams has had a fruitful experience with lithography. On one of his visits to Taos in the late twenties, B. J. O. Nordfeldt admired certain of Adams' drawings and suggested that they would make fine lithographic prints. He gave Adams several zinc plates and some crayons that he was not going to use. With these Adams produced four lithographs: *Albidia, Taos Indian Woman, Washerwoman* and *New Mexico Village Under Snow.* The Western Lithograph Company of Wichita, Kansas, printed these. Later George C. Miller of New York City, who had printed many of George Bellows lithographs, printed for Adams *Taos Indian Girl, Ranchos Church—Moonlight, The Spring* and *House in the Sun.*

Elmer Schooley of New Mexico Highlands University also printed a group of lithographs from Adams' stones: *Francisca, Taos Indian, Old Taos Indian, Vieja Taoseña, The Card Players* and *Benerisa.*

It is interesting to note that in every instance where an Adams lithograph and painting incorporate the same motif, the lithograph preceded the painting. This is an unusual procedure for a painter.

In both drawings and lithographs a natural facility for bold draftsmanship preserves the factual elements while assembling a range of shapes which also have strength from a formal point of view.

Adams could have depended upon his distinctive talent for integrating lines and a broad treatment of essentials. This would have made it easy to shape his style along lines that would charm through sheer naturalism. Instead we often find areas of pigment in which he has conveyed a sense of reality without actually copying the model as it appeared before him. His perceptive treatment of the relationship between various masses imbues these pictures with a stark but imposing quality.

We feel the basic sobriety of the Indian and Spanish peoples through his broad plastic representations. His landscapes engage our attention through bright and imaginative use of nondescriptive color. When painting flowers he brings to each petal a gamut of hues that balances botanical with pictorial considerations. In all these subjects painterly values of a sensuous quality dominate rudimentary reality.

Paramount is the way in which Adams indicates a genuine affection for his subjects even when maintaining a detachment ruled by aesthetic judgments. He extracts from the bewildering multiplicity of nature a sensitive selected unity of ordered forms and fresh color harmonies. These simple arrangements exist as a symbol of the man, a period of time, and a special environment.

VAN DEREN COKE

CATALOG OF THE EXHIBITION

4

[This catalog was prepared for a retrospective exhibition of Kenneth M. Adams' work at The Art Gallery, University of New Mexico, March 31 through May 3, 1964. In the dimensions given, height precedes width. The numbers with the illustrations refer to the numbers in this catalog list.]

OIL PAINTINGS

1. FRENCH LANDSCAPE. 1922. 19x25 in. Collection of the artist.
2. INDIAN GIRL WITH BASKET OF CORN. 1924. 32x25 in. Dr. and Mrs. Joseph Gordon, Albuquerque.
3. WALPI. 1924. 24x30 in. Mrs. Faye Davison, Wichita.
4. INDIAN WOMAN AND CHILD. 1925. 40x36 in. Caprock Hotel, Lubbock.
5. PORTRAIT OF A PIONEER. 1925. 40x36 in. Mr. and Mrs. Orvil Shreeves, Taos.
6. OLD WOMAN. 1926. 51x41 in. Caprock Hotel, Lubbock.
7. AUTUMN LANDSCAPE. C. 1926. 18x24 in. Collection of the artist.
8. DOÑA ASCENCIONE IN WICKER CHAIR. 1927. 32x32 in. Joslyn Art Museum, Omaha.
9. TALPA LANDSCAPE. 1929. 18x24 in. Dr. and Mrs. S. W. Wiest, Albuquerque.
10. BENERISA TAFOYA. 1932. 32x25 in. International Business Machines Corporation, New York.
11. PORTRAIT OF A BOY. 1933. 30x24 in. Wichita High School East, Wichita.
12. PORTRAIT OF JUAN DURAN. 1933. 40x30 in. United States Department of Labor, Washington, D.C.
13. CHURCH AT SAN ANTONITO. 1934. 30x40 in. University of New Mexico.

61

8

14. NEW MEXICO LANDSCAPE. 1934. 40x36 in. Mr. Albert G. Simms, Albuquerque.

15. PORTRAIT OF HILDA. 1934. 40x30 in. Museum of New Mexico, Santa Fe.

16. PORTRAIT OF A NATIVE GIRL. 1934. 40x36 in. Kansas State University, Manhattan.

17. PEACHES. 1936. 12x16 in. Mr. and Mrs. L. E. Perkins, Albuquerque.

18. JUANITA. c. 1938. 30x24 in. Collection of the artist.

19. FRUIT STILL LIFE. 1940. 24x30 in. Dr. and Mrs. John W. Myers, Albuquerque.

20. WHITE ROSES. 1940. 20x16 in. Miss Irene Ormsby, Albuquerque.

21. YELLOW TULIPS. 1942. 20x16 in. Dr. Harry Bryant, Albuquerque.

22. CLARA. 1943. 24x30 in. Collection of the artist.

23. LANDSCAPE. 1945. 18x30 in. Mrs. Frances L. Newcomb, Albuquerque.

24. HARVEST. 1946. 40x36 in. Collection of the artist.

25. THE SPRING. 1946. 30x24 in. Dr. and Mrs. L. V. Broadbent, Cedar City, Utah.

26. FRUIT WITH EGG PLANT. 1947. 18x30 in. Mr. and Mrs. Frank Quinn, Albuquerque.

27. PINK TULIPS. 1950. 24x18 in. Mr. and Mrs. Saul Harberg, Taos.

28. HONDO CANYON—EVENING. 1952. 24x18 in. Miss Myrtle Greenfield, Albuquerque.

29. THE VALLEY. 1952. 30x40 in. Collection of the artist.

30. THE VALLEY—RAIN. 1952. 18x24 in. Mrs. Joan Florance, Albuquerque.

31. WHITE TULIPS. 1954. 30x24 in. Mr. and Mrs. M. M. Prinkey, Albuquerque.

10

11

32. ZINNIAS. 1954. 24x20 in. Dr. and Mrs. W. W. Hill, Albuquerque.
33. ZINNIAS. 1955. 20x24 in. Mr. and Mrs. Jack F. Walton, Albuquerque.
34. INDIAN HEAD. 1956. 20x16 in. Mr. and Mrs. Edwin Sackett, Albuquerque.
35. LADY MOHR IRIS. 1956. 16x21 in. Mr. and Mrs. J. R. Modrall, Albuquerque.
36. SEATED NUDE. 1956. 24x18 in. Collection of the artist.
37. ZINNIAS. 1956. 20x16 in. Mr. and Mrs. Edwin Sackett, Albuquerque.
38. FLAMINGO IRIS. 1957. 24x18 in. Mr. and Mrs. Homer Schlamer, Albuquerque.
39. IRIS. 1957. 24x16 in. Collection of the artist.
40. MAROON ZINNIAS. 1957. 30x24 in. Dr. and Mrs. Joseph Gordon, Albuquerque.
41. PORTRAIT OF COLONEL D. C. PEARSON. 1957. 30x24 in. New Mexico Military Institute, Roswell.
42. SLEEPING MODEL. 1957. 24x42 in. Collection of the artist.

House in the Sun   Kenneth M. Adams

12

14

43. MIXED ZINNIAS. 1958. 24x30 in. Collection of the artist.
44. PINK ROSES. 1958. 20x16 in. Mr. and Mrs. Thomas J. McCaffrey, Albuquerque.
45. RED ROSES. 1959. 16x12 in. Mrs. R. H. Gass, Albuquerque.
46. YELLOW ZINNIAS AND WHITE DAISIES. 1959. 24x18 in. Mr. and Mrs. Jack Wentworth, Albuquerque.
47. LAVENDER ZINNIAS. 1960. 24x18 in. Collection of the artist.
48. PORTRAIT OF PAT. 1961. 30x24 in. Collection of the artist.
49. ASTERS, PETUNIAS AND DAISIES. 1962. 30x24 in. Collection of the artist.
50. BENERISA. 1962. 20x16 in. Collection of the artist.
51. PORTRAIT OF MRS. W. C. BATES. 1962. 40x36 in. Mr. and Mrs. W. C. Bates, Albuquerque.

WATERCOLORS

52. LANDSCAPE. 1930. 9¾x17 in. Frank Reeve, Albuquerque.
53. LANDSCAPE. 1935. 12x19 in. Mrs. Raymond Ryan, Albuquerque.
54. GOUACHE. 1944. 18x13 in. Collection of the artist.
55. LUCIA. 1945. 15¾x12½ in. Mrs. Jane Hiatt, Taos.
56. TAOS INDIAN WOMAN. 1946. 28x17 in. Mr. and Mrs. Louis G. Bradley, Albuquerque.
57. HONDO PALISADES NO. 1. 1952. 14x20 in. Collection of the artist.
58. HONDO PALISADES NO. 2. 1952. 14x20 in. Collection of the artist.

16

DRAWINGS

59. NUDE BACK. 1919. Red conté, 12½x9½ in. Collection of the artist.
60. CLEOFA, INDIAN HEAD. 1926. Pencil, 12x10 in. Mrs. O. E. Berninghaus, Taos.
61. REYCITA BERNAL. 1926. Pencil, 13½x12¼ in. University of New Mexico, gift of Andrew Dasburg.
62. ROBERTO—STUDY FOR A PORTRAIT. 1926. Pencil, 15x20 in. Mr. and Mrs. W. C. Bates, Albuquerque.
63. RANCHOS ROAD—WINTER. 1932. Charcoal, 9¼x14½ in. Mrs. Frank H. Kentnor, Taos.
64. SANDIA MOUNTAINS IN SNOW. 1945. Sauce crayon, 11x20½ in. Collection of the artist
65. NORTHERN MOUNTAINS. 1955. Black and red conté, 13¼x20½ in. Mrs. Jane Hiatt, Taos.
66. "MICHELLE"—NUDE TORSO. 1956. Black sauce crayon, 26x19 in. Mr. and Mrs. Jack Wentworth, Albuquerque.
67. BENERISA. 1960. Charcoal, 16x12 in. Collection of the artist.

LITHOGRAPHS

68. NEW MEXICO UNDER SNOW. Edition 40, 1929. 13½x8 in. Collection of the artist.
69. OLD NATIVE WOMAN (small head). Edition 40, 1929. 10½x7 in. Collection of the artist.
70. OLD TAOS INDIAN (small head). Edition 40, 1929. 10x7 in. Mr. and Mrs. Robert Hopewell, Albuquerque.
71. WASHERWOMEN. Edition 30, 1929. 15½x13 in. Collection of the artist.
72. ALBIDIA. Edition 50, 1930. 18x11½ in. Mr. and Mrs. Robert Hopewell, Albuquerque.

25

85

73. TAOS INDIAN WOMAN. Edition 40, 1930. 11x8 in. Mr. and Mrs. Robert Hopewell, Albuquerque.

74. ADOBE WORKERS. Edition 50, 1931. 14x10 in. Collection of the artist.

75. RANCHOS DE TAOS CHURCH—MOONLIGHT. Edition 30, 1931. 9x10¾ in. Miss Myrtle Greenfield, Albuquerque.

76. DOÑA ASCENCIONE. Edition 50, 1932. 11½x9½ in. Miss Myrtle Greenfield, Albuquerque.

77. TAOS INDIAN GIRL. Edition 50, 1932. 8¼x10½ in. Collection of the artist.

78. HOUSE IN THE SUN. Edition 50, 1933. 9½x16¾ in. Collection of the artist.

79. WOMAN'S HEAD. Edition 50, 1933. 12x8 in. Collection of the artist.

80. ADOBE BRICK MAKER. Edition 50, 1934. 9¼x10 in. Collection of the artist.

81. WINTER. Edition 40, 1934. 7½x8½ in. Collection of the artist.

82. THE MINER. Edition 50, 1937. 15x9¼ in. University of New Mexico.

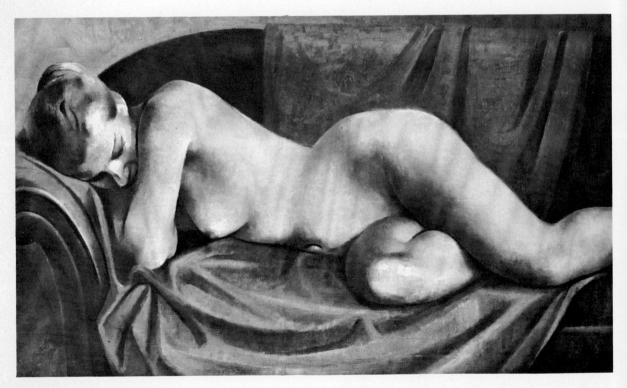

39

83. HARVEST. Edition 100, 1940. 11x9 in. Mr. and
Mrs. Robert Hopewell, Albuquerque.
84. THE SPRING. Edition 100, 1946. 14¾x11½ in.
Mr. and Mrs. J. R. Modrall, Albuquerque.
85. VIEJA TAOSEÑA. Edition 60, 1952. 16½x13 in.
Mr. and Mrs. Tom Popejoy, Albuquerque.
86. FRANCISCA. Edition 100, 1954. 15¼x12 in. Mr.
and Mrs. Edward Clingenpeel, Albuquerque.
87. OLD TAOS INDIAN. (large). Edition 100, 1956.
14x11 in. Mr. and Mrs. Edward Clingenpeel,
Albuquerque.
88. TAOS INDIAN. (profile). Edition 100, 1957.
16x12¼ in. Collection of the artist.
89. CARD PLAYERS. Edition 100, 1959. 17½x23 in.
Collection of the artist.
90. BENERISA. Edition 20, 1960. 16x12 in. Miss
Myrtle Greenfield, Albuquerque.

43

48

CHRONOLOGY

1897 August 6: Kenneth Miller Adams born in Topeka, Kansas, the youngest of six children. Attends the public schools of Topeka where he receives instruction in the rudiments of perspective drawing and watercolor painting. Spends spare time poring over the few badly-illustrated art books in the public library from which he tries to copy the work of popular magazine illustrators.

In high school takes course called "Freehand Drawing" and works in charcoal from costumed models for the first time. His teacher, noting his interest, encourages him to seek further instruction. He persuades his father to let him take private lessons from George M. Stone, a local portrait painter, who had studied in Paris with LeFebvre and Boulanger. Stone teaches him to paint in oils from still life and portrait models.

1916 In the autumn enters classes at the Art Institute of Chicago. There for the first time sees paintings by the masters as well as exhibitions by contemporary American and European painters. In the spring of 1917 the school is disrupted by the entrance of the United States into World War I. Returns to Topeka and takes a job as timekeeper for a building contractor.

In September, 1918, is drafted into the United States Army and serves at Camp Funston, Kansas, until honorably discharged in December of the same year.

1919 Goes to New York in the early spring and enrolls at the Art Students League of New York in the classes of George B. Bridgeman and Kenneth Hayes Miller. In the De Zayas Gallery sees a drawing of a nude torso by Andrew Dasburg which impresses him so much that he enters Dasburg's class at the Art Students League summer school at Woodstock, New York. Here he paints all summer from nude models posed out-of-doors. At Woodstock makes the acquaintance of the painters Birge Harrison, John F. Carlson, George Bellows, Leon Kroll, Eugene Speicher, Henry Lee McFee, Charles Rosen and Henry Mattson. Among his other associates are the commercial artists Cushman Parker, Frank Chase, Edward L. Chase, Dean Cornwell and Jay Hyde Barnum.

Dasburg encourages Adams to pursue a career in the fine arts rather than in commercial art. In the autumn returns to the Art Students League in New York and enters the classes of Maurice Sterne and Eugene Speicher. The following summer returns to Dasburg's class at Woodstock.

1921 Remains in Woodstock, painting independently until the summer. In July of that year goes to Paris, France. There studies the paintings in the museums and commercial galleries. At the Louvre the paintings of Delacroix, Ingres, Daumier, Courbet, Corot, and Manet attract his attention. In the commercial galleries he sees the work of Matisse, Picasso, Braque, Bonnard, Dufy, Rouault, Derain, Vlaminck, Utrillo, and Segonzac.

At the Academie Ransom, draws extensively from the nude. In the autumn joins his friend, Ward Lockwood, and Alexander Warshawsky at Villeneuve-les-Avignon in Provence. With them paints the landscape and in December moves to the warmer climate of Cassis-Sur-Mer.

1922 In April returns to Villeneuve-les-Avignon, working there until July when he again goes to Paris. Returns to Villeneuve-les-Avignon in the autumn of 1922 and paints there through January, 1923. In February makes a trip to Italy where he studies the art of that country for the next three months. Returning to Villeneuve-les-Avignon, paints the Provençal landscape. This experience greatly enhances his appreciation of the work of Corot, Cézanne, and Van Gogh. In July goes to Paris and after a stay of two weeks returns to the United States. In the autumn of 1923 exhibits his paintings of the south of France at the Findlay Gallery in Kansas City, Missouri, and later that same year at the Mulvane Museum in Topeka, Kansas.

1924 In February joins his friend and former teacher, Andrew Dasburg at Santa Fe, New Mexico. Unable to find adequate studio and living quarters there, he goes to Taos with a letter of introduction from Dasburg to Walter Ufer. Ufer generously aids him to establish a studio adjacent to his own on Pueblo Road and introduces him to other resident artists. Begins to paint the Taos Pueblo Indians. Early attempts at New Mexico landscapes are frustrated by the immensity of the country and the brilliance of the light.

Ufer builds a studio nearer to his residence and Adams moves into the vacated quarters in order to have a larger place to work.

1927 Moves to a house and studio on Ledoux Street in Taos, next door to the Harwood Foundation. Is elected to the Taos Society of Artists, the youngest and last member to join this famous art organization.

1928 In July marries Hilda Brann Boulton, after which they occupy an apartment and studio in the Harwood Foundation.

In October has first and only New York "one-man show" at the Ferargil Gallery on West 57th Street.

1930 In the spring, leases and remodels an old adobe house located on what was then the Las Vegas highway, about a mile from the village of Ranchos de Taos. The Spanish Americans become the dominant subject of his paintings and lithographs, along with a renewed interest in landscape painting.

1933 Teaches the autumn semester at the University of New Mexico in Albuquerque. While he had taught at the University's Field School of Art in Taos every summer from its inception in 1929, this was the first experience with formal university teaching. At this time the United States Government, concerned with the economic plight of the artist, establishes an art project under the direction of the Treasury Department. Through this agency money is made available to hire artists on a weekly basis to paint murals and easel paintings and make prints. Gustave Baumann of Santa Fe, the regional director of this project, places Adams on the payroll at the top wage of $42.50 a week. This makes it possible to return to Ranchos de Taos and devote entire time to painting. While on this project, executes one lithograph, several watercolors and a group of portraits and landscapes in oil. The murals of Rivera, Orozco, and Siqueiros afford technical information about large scale compositions and influences the style of Adams' work. He executes two murals, one for the Post Office at Goodland, Kansas, and the other for the Post Office at Deming, New Mexico, under the art project of the Treasury Department.

1935 Adams, Dasburg, and Lockwood commissioned to decorate with murals the theater lounge of the Colorado Springs Fine Arts Center. Adams executes there the composition titled "Ballet."

1938 In March is elected an Associate of the National Academy of Design.

In the autumn begins a two-year program as Artist-in-Residence at the University of New Mexico supported by a grant from the Carnegie Corporation of New York. Begins four murals for the University Library which are completed in 1939.

1940 Made head of the Art Department of Sandia School, Albuquerque, New Mexico, a private school for girls established by Mrs. Albert C. Simms. Continues in this capacity until 1942 when the school is abandoned and the property sold to the United States Government. Continues as a member of the faculty of the University of New Mexico. Production during the 1939-1948 decade is somewhat limited due to the time devoted to teaching and the care of his wife. Wife dies in December, 1948.

1949 Adams marries Helen Asborn Hogrefe. Directs the University's Field School of Art at Taos, for the summer session in 1950, 1951 and 1952. During this period becomes particularly interested in flowers as a motif. This subject has a strong appeal due to intense color and unusual combinations of hues. Many paintings of zinnias are executed when he finds they retain their form and color longer than most flowers.

While continuing his interest in the Taos Indian and rural Spanish-American residents of Ranchos de Taos, the greater part of his production in Albuquerque is devoted to drawings and paintings of the nude, portraits, and still lifes.

1950 The University of New Mexico Press publishes a portfolio of eight reproductions of Adams' lithographs.

1961 An Associate member of the National Academy of Design since 1938, Adams is elected an Academician.

1963 Is elected to the Honor Society, Phi Kappa Phi. Retires as a professor at the University of New Mexico.

Two works included in *Taos and Santa Fe: The Artist's Environment, 1882-1942,* an exhibition organized by The Art Gallery, University of New Mexico, in cooperation with the Amon Carter Museum of Western Art, Ft. Worth.

1964 Large-scale retrospective exhibition held in The Art Gallery, University of New Mexico.

BIBLIOGRAPHY AND HONORS

Kenneth M. Adams: Portfolio of Lithographs. Albuquerque, University of New Mexico Press, 1950.

Coke, Van Deren. *Taos and Santa Fe: The Artist's Environment, 1882-1942.* pp. 39, 68, 89, 97, 119, 122, 124, 126, 127, 152. Albuquerque, University of New Mexico Press, 1963.

Goff, Lloyd Lózes. Kenneth M. Adams. *New Mexico Artists.* pp. 51-63. Albuquerque, University of New Mexico Press, 1952.

Honors: Elected to National Academy of Design, 1961.

Murals: Goodland, Kansas, Post Office, 1936, *Rural Free Delivery;* Colorado Springs, Colorado, Fine Arts Center, 1936, *Ballet;* Deming, New Mexico, Post Office, 1937, *Mountains and Yucca;* University of New Mexico, Library, four murals, winter, 1938-39, *The Peoples of New Mexico.*

WORKS IN PUBLIC COLLECTIONS

Albuquerque: University of New Mexico, *Church at San Antonito; New Mexico Landscape.* New Mexico Art League, Albuquerque Public Library, *Taos Street.*

Lubbock: Caprock Hotel, *Indian Woman and Child; Old Woman.*

Manhattan: Kansas State University, *Portrait of a Native Girl.*

New York: International Business Machines Corporation, *Benerisa Tafoya.*

Omaha, Nebraska: Joslyn Art Museum, *Doña Ascensione in Wicker Chair.*

Roswell: New Mexico Military Institute, *Portrait of Colonel D. C. Pearson.*

Santa Fe: Museum of New Mexico, *Portrait of Hilda.*

Taos, New Mexico: The Harwood Foundation, *Muchacho.*

Washington, D.C.: The United States Department of Labor, *Portrait of Juan Duran.*

Wichita, Kansas: Wichita High School East, *Portrait of a Boy.*